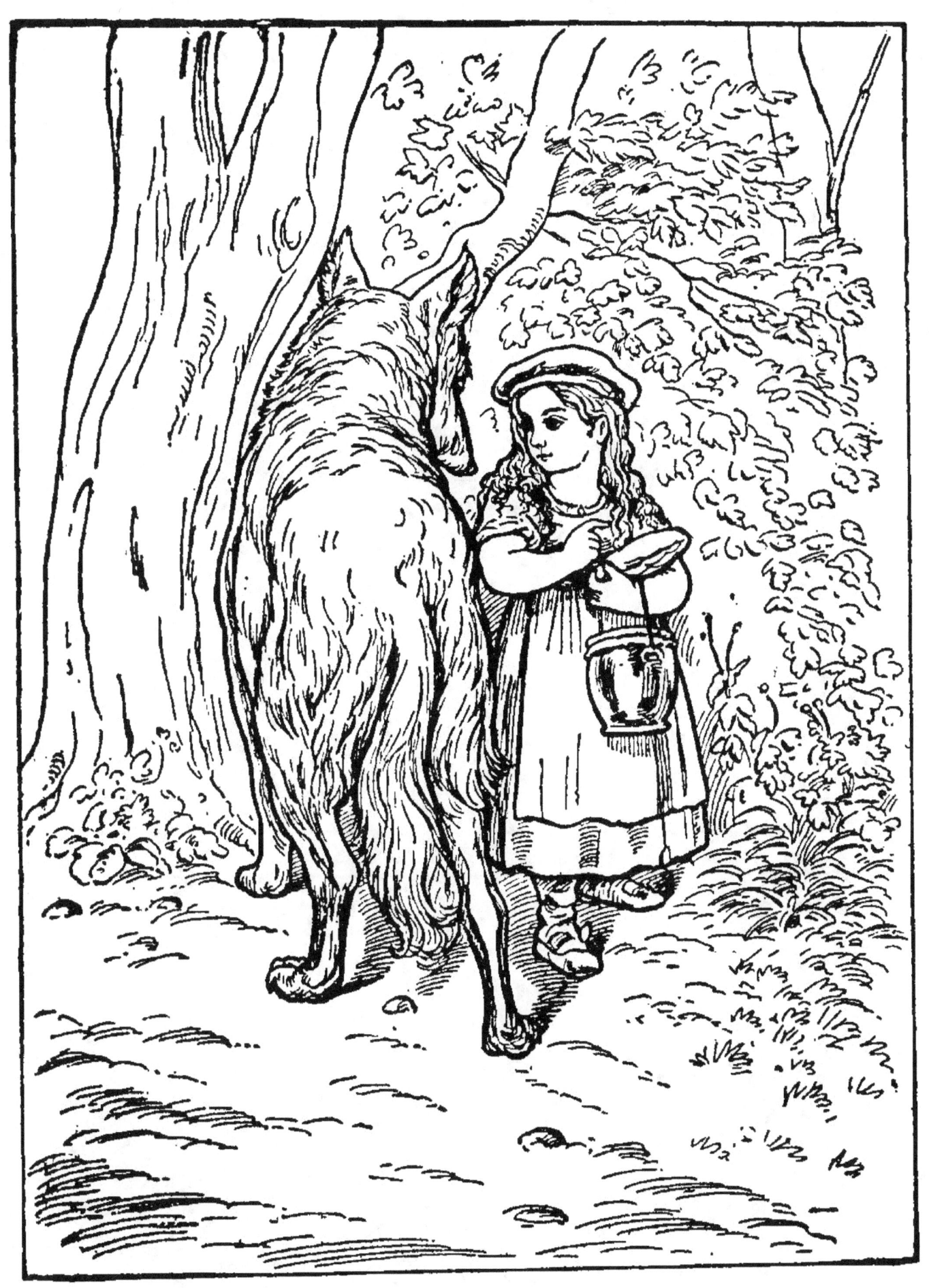

"SHE MET WITH GAFFER WOLF."

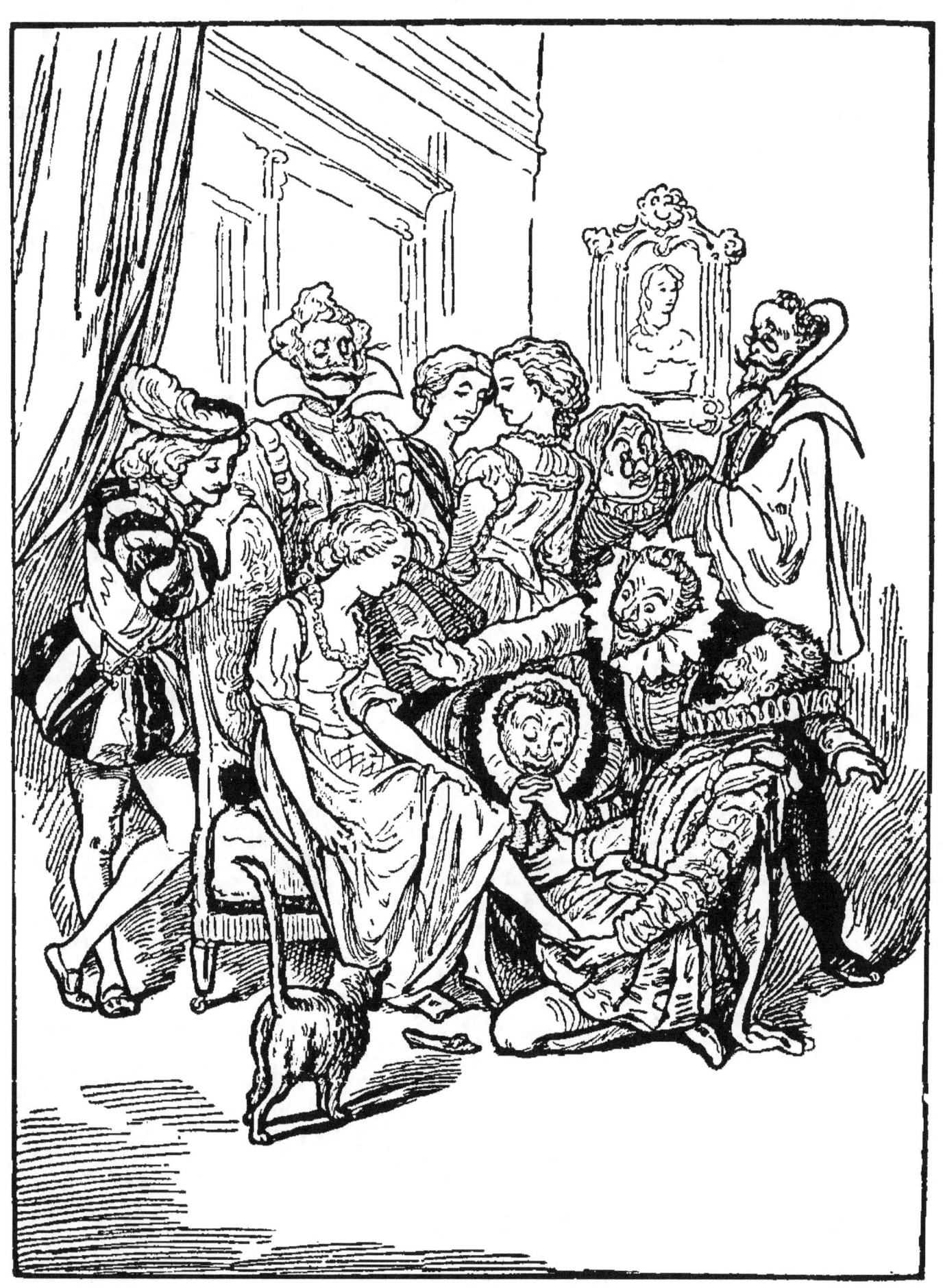

"IT WENT ON VERY EASILY."

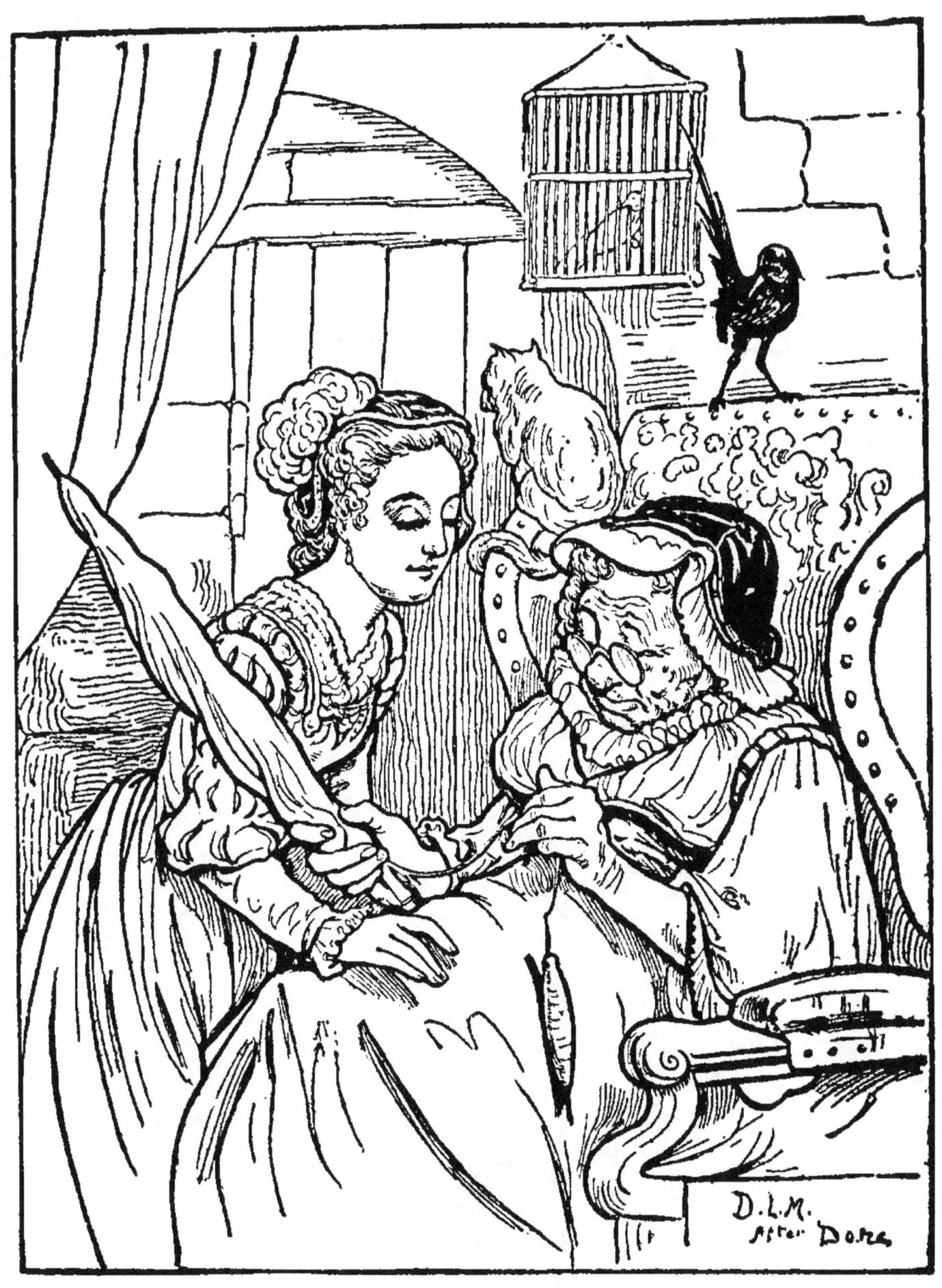

"LET ME SEE IF I CAN DO IT."

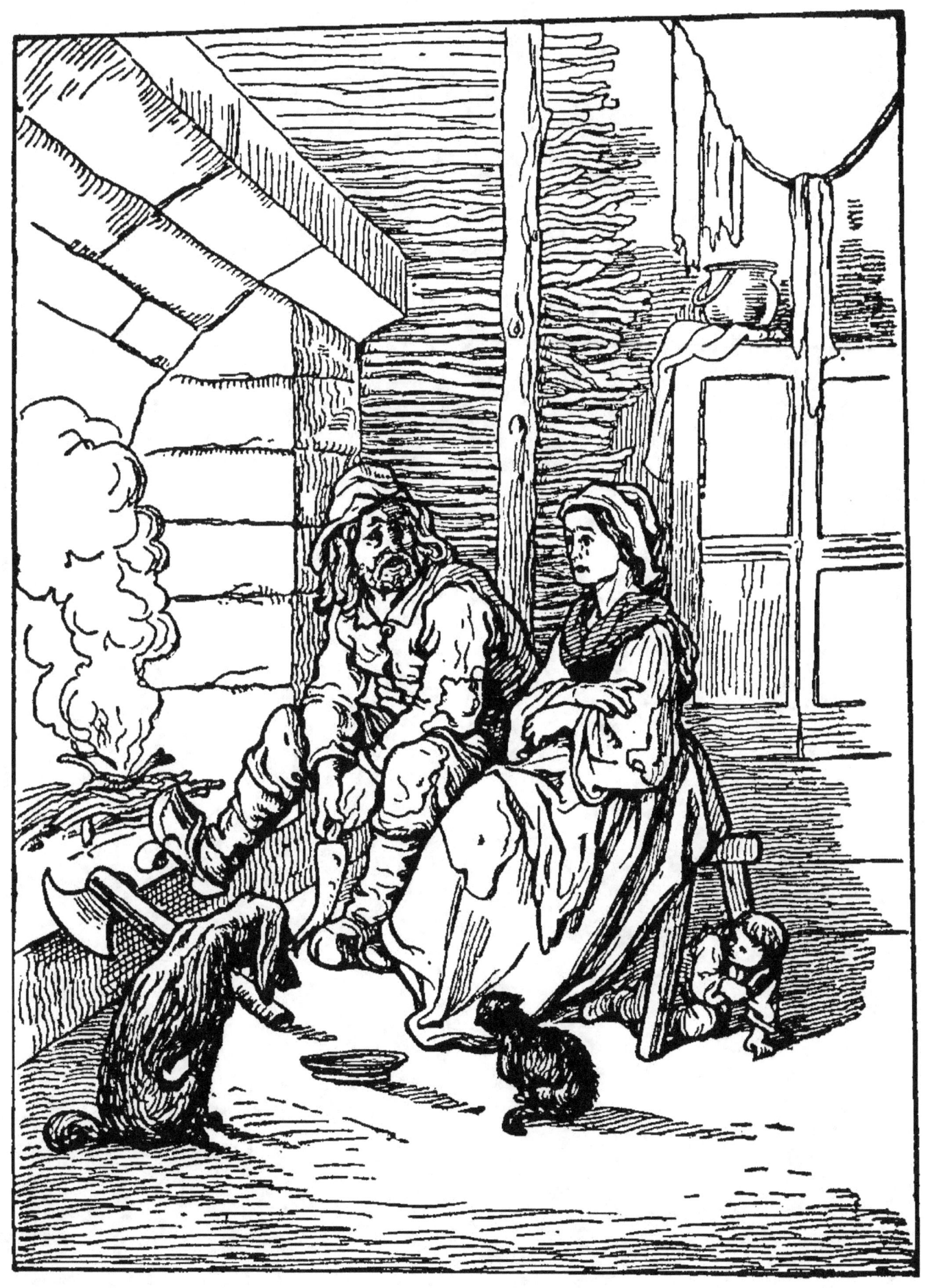

"SLIPPED UNDER HIS FATHER'S SEAT."

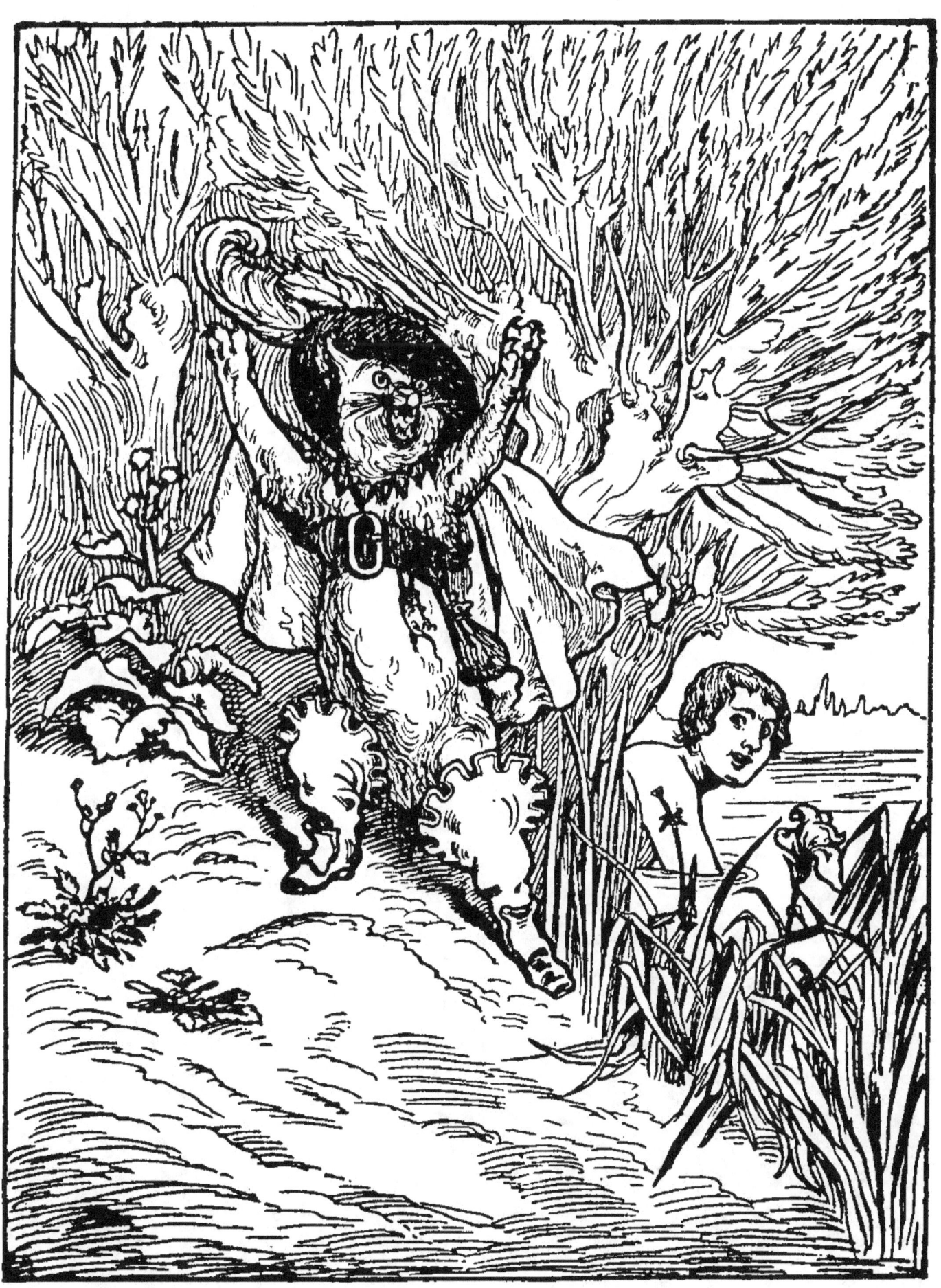

"The Marquis of Carabas is drowning!"

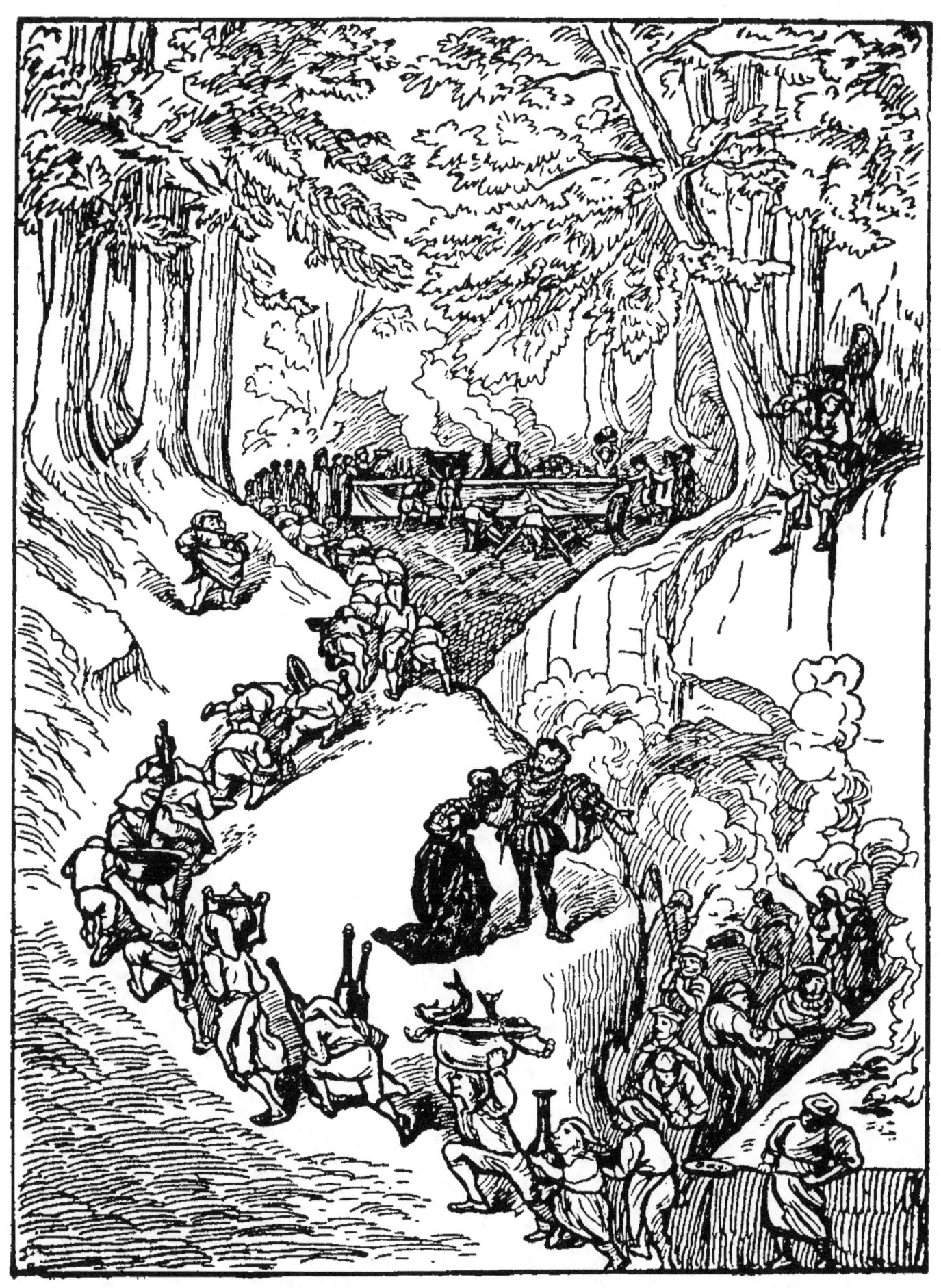

"I AM EXACT IN KEEPING MY WORD."

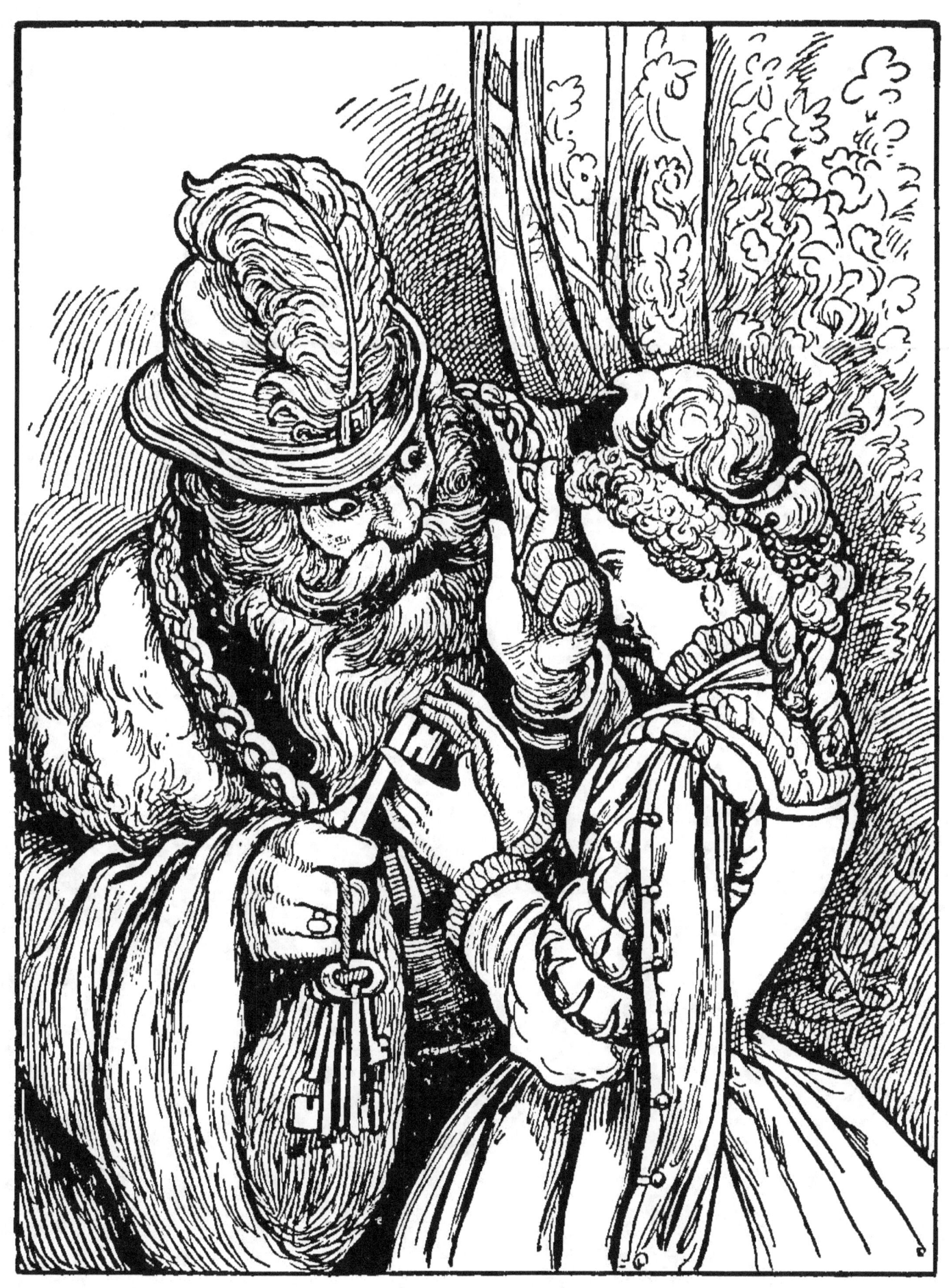

"IF YOU OPEN IT, THERE'S NOTHING YOU MAY NOT EXPECT FROM MY ANGER."

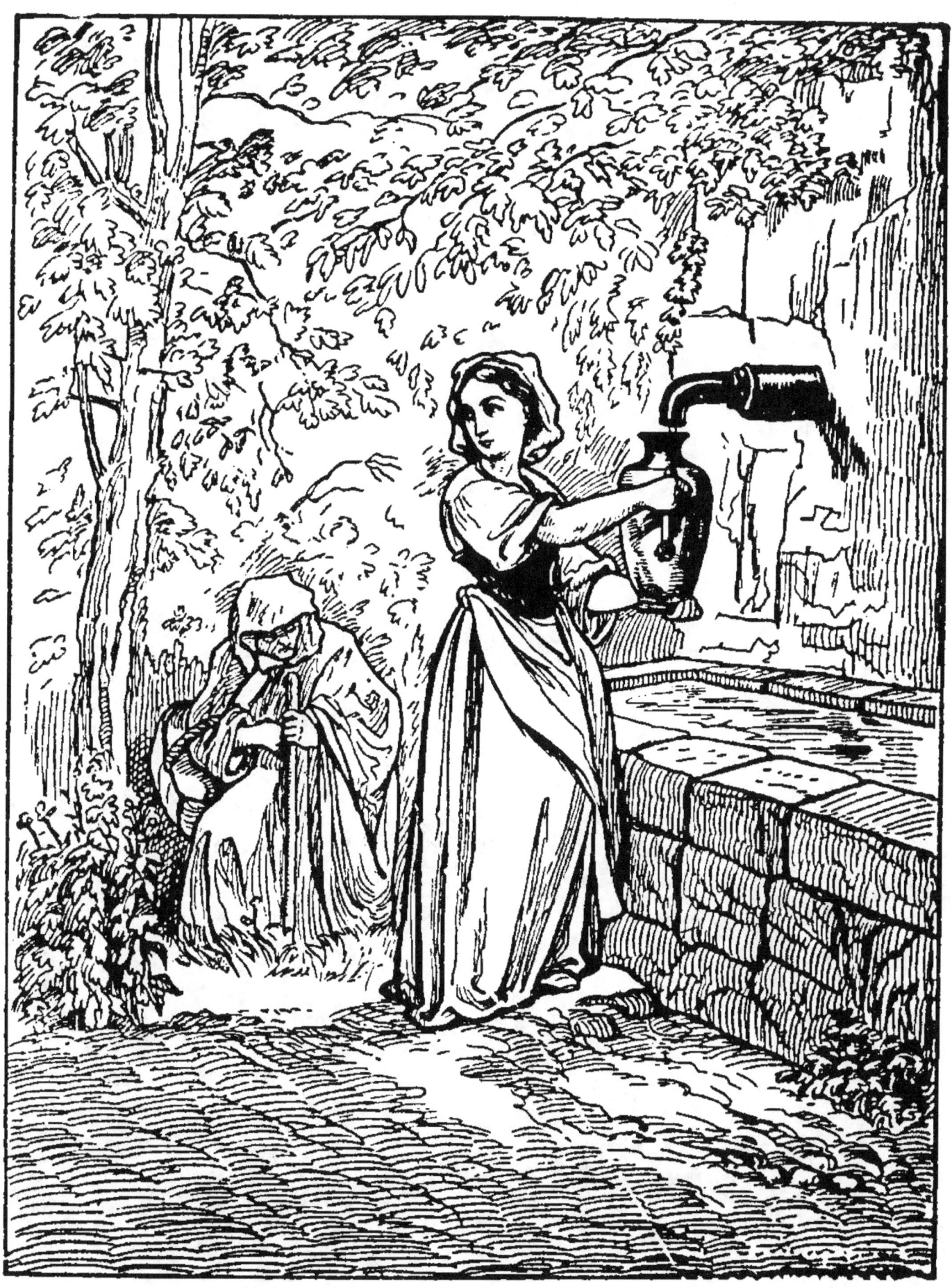

"WITH ALL MY HEART, GOODY."

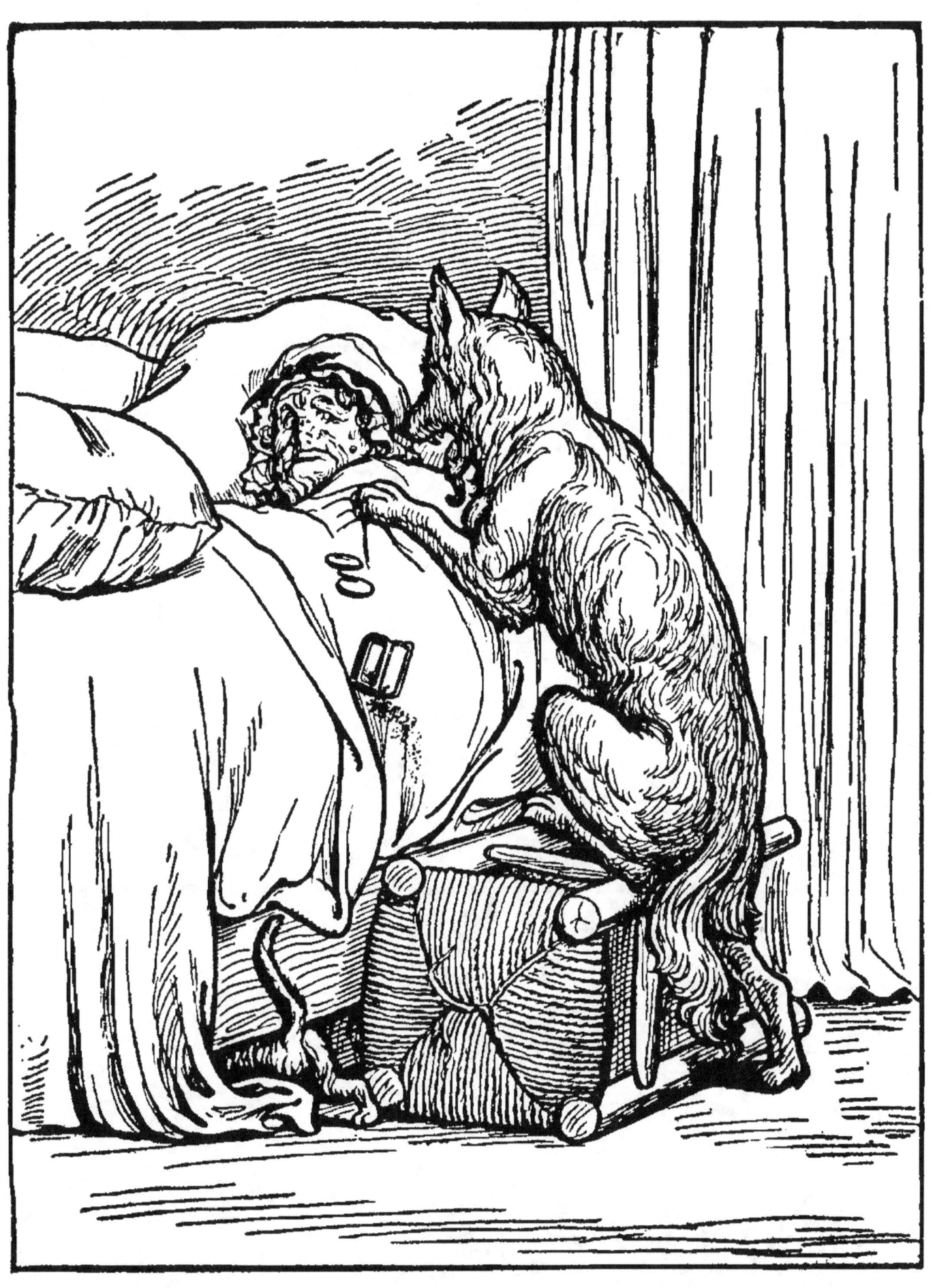

"HE FELL UPON THE GOOD WOMAN."